JUDO
GAMES

Other books available from A & C Black:

EP Sport Judo by Geof Gleeson
Health and Fitness in the Martial Arts
    by Dr J. C. Canney
Judo Inside Out by Geof Gleeson
Know the Game Judo by Geof Gleeson
The Martial Arts Coaching Manual
    by David Mitchell

JUDO GAMES

GEOF GLEESON

A & C Black · London

First published 1989 by
A & C Black (Publishers) Ltd
35 Bedford Row, London WC1R 4JH

© 1989 Geof Gleeson

ISBN 0 7136 5709 X

A CIP catalogue record for this book is
available from the British Library.

Photoset by Rowland Phototypesetting Ltd
Bury St Edmunds, Suffolk
Printed and bound in Great Britain by
The Amadeus Press Ltd, Huddersfield,
West Yorkshire

Contents

Why games?

What is judo?

What is judo? The question is asked not in the context of history or philosophy, but simply in terms of expectation. What does judo expect from people who wish to participate in it? What sort of person is needed? What sort of talent is called for? What sort of physical attributes are required? To a great extent the answer depends upon the aspirations of the individual taking part in judo. Does he want to do it for fun, or to become an international competitor?

I shall be assuming he is doing it for top performance. Why? Top physical performance is somewhat analogous to a racing car: the very importance of its design, the pressures for maintaining excellence and the stress produced by sustained high performance throw the needs of the family saloon into stark relief. The same is true of judo performance: by studying the needs of the champion, the needs of the novice in the way of training and preparation become clearer than in any text book.

Yet, to answer this kind of 'What is judo?' question is still very difficult. If I tried to make a comprehensive 'shopping list' of all the qualities I think a 'good' judo competitor should have, I would be bound to omit some. Worse than that, I would be implying that if the individual did not have all, or most, of those qualities, he could not be a 'good' judo fighter. The truth is, a champion makes the best of what he has; that may be most of the qualities I would list, or very few of them. One of the purposes of training is to exploit and develop whatever innate qualities the ambitious competitor already has, for the maximum effect in the minimum amount of time.

After all, top performance is frequently a matter of compensation. If an individual lacks some supposed essential characteristic, he may well deliberately cultivate some other unique characteristic of his own which will more than outweigh the supposed benefits of the traditional factors. For example, several years ago flexibility was said to be the essential quality of a top judo man. At that time, Brian Jacks and David Starbrook were contemporaries in international competition; because Jacks was much more flexible than Starbrook, it was often said that he was therefore the better judo man – in spite of Starbrook's formidable list of successes. Even Starbrook's coach tried to make him more flexible, and in doing so possibly made him less effective. Starbrook's inflexibility

7

was, in more ways than one, his strength. It was an essential part of his skill. Change it and you risked weakening that skill altogether.

What is skill?
Here is the nub of the matter. What is skill? We can usually appreciate it, but we seldom understand it.

In practical terms we know how it happens – it is a response (by the performer) to a set of ephemeral circumstances that if manipulated accurately will allow the competitor to do what he wants to do. The better the performer, the better he can exploit these circumstances, and the greater degree of success to be expected. However, by description and by performance the skill will be unique to that individual and that set of circumstances only.

In theory it is nowhere near that simple. When we look at the working performance, we have to ask such questions as, 'How does the man recognise the right set of circumstances, as a situation he can react to, so that he can do what he wants to do?'

Syncretistic vision
Starting from such a mystical enigma, there are bound to be many explanations on offer. Their validity will depend upon the wisdom and experience of the explicator. The notion I prefer (at the moment; it may change again next year!) is that which can be called 'comparative dynamic imagery'. The idea is that the performer builds up a store of blurred, fuzzy images of various actions he has done at one time or another. All of these are very dynamic and do much the same job, i.e. throw a man. When he meets a new, unknown set of circumstances in which he has to throw a man, he is able instantly to relate and compare that situation to his store of experienced dynamic images, and from that store create something spontaneously for the new set of circumstances.

In the trade of perception this is known as 'syncretistic vision' and is probably why artists advocate (to their apprentices) looking at the subject to be painted through almost closed eyes. Such a view shatters the contour lines and blurs the form – and thus allows the 'scattered' pieces to be brought back together in new forms.

Piaget used the word 'dedifferentiated imagery', describing how an image is 'scattered across the ego', allowing other images – contemporary, past and possibly even future* – to interact and produce new dynamic solutions to the problems being faced.

'Exactness' is not a part of this process. It is not necessary, or even desirable, for the trainee to see precisely what he is looking at. He wants just enough reality to excite him to create new images and actions – which are the same thing.

---

*Read F. Hoyle's *The Intelligent Universe*.

Certainly, artists know about syncretistic vision, even if they have never met the words.

> A picture is not thought out and settled beforehand. While it is being done it changes as one's thoughts change. And when it is finished, it still goes on changing, according to the state of mind of whoever is looking at it.
>
> Pablo Picasso

> Painting is a method of representation. One must not imitate what one wants to create. One does not imitate appearances; the appearance is the result. To be pure imitation, painting must forget appearance. To work from nature is to improvise.
>
> Georges Braque

Skill and technique

However, coaches, especially judo coaches, have never heard of syncretistic vision – either by word or deed. They are under the impression that skills, or their preferred word, technique, can only be reproduced or learned by precise imitation of what has gone before. How Braque would disagree. They say each successive generation must conform to the same archetypal action laid down by tradition. Before an action is to be tried, it must always be thought out and settled. Picasso could not agree with that! Sometimes, of course, that is necessary, but not always.

Much time has been wasted in the judo world by trying to replicate an exact, imposed movement. For a good example, one has only to look at the practice of uchikomi: an exercise with the intention of reproducing an exact copy of only a *part* of a throwing technique, not even all of it. That must be redundant ambition for competition, although if treated as kata it may have some value. (More about that later.)

Technique, as a rigid form of a permanent 'basic technique', has no existence. Technique is merely a way of doing something, but it has no permanence. It is a way that can be analysed for short term improvement, but can be totally divorced from reality, or contains so little as to mislead the analyst. That is why I prefer to use the word 'skill': a response to a real situation, however ephemeral; a response that is a mixture of past experience and future fantasy.

To create something spontaneously new out of a micro-second of void will require an ability to fantasise. The training programme will need special set-aside-periods in which the trainees can learn to create fantastically and in doing so receive positive encouragement from the coaches.

So, how are ever-changing skills to be taught? If every uchimata that is done by the same person is different – and it is – how can he be taught all those ways? It is a tough challenge; many coaches do opt out and teach one type of uchimata to everybody, and hope that each individual can modify it to suit his own qualities. That job is, of course, made very much harder if, at the same time, the coach is insisting that his 'technique' is the only legitimate one.

If the coach, on the other hand, were to suggest that his 'technique' was only a rough model and must be modified immediately by each individual if it is going to work for him, the chances of stimulating originality in terms of success might be greater. (The chances would be even greater if the trainee had been lucky enough to avoid attending a beginners' course.) However, to achieve originality is not easy, and more constructive guide-lines will usually be necessary. Let us look at some.

Note

Throughout the book coaches and trainees are, in the main, referred to individually as 'he'. This should, of course, be taken to mean 'he or she' where appropriate.

Is judo art?

Using words such as creativity, originality, fantasy and imitation recalls the hoary old question, 'Is judo art?' To discuss briefly the question may help us to see how, or indeed if, we can learn from the answer, and to assist us sort out some games for the development of originality.

Deciding whether judo is or is not art depends to a great extent on the definition of art chosen for judgement. If the definition is largely concerned with the aesthetics of movement and the harmony of action, then perhaps it could be squeezed in. If the definition is concerned largely with spontaneous creativity or divergent thinking, then the answer would be no. The definition of art I prefer – because it is my own – is:

> The translation of one form of reality into another (form) in the first instance for the benefit of the translator (e.g. artist), in the second for the benefit of the observer.

Such a definition infers learning, training, study and education, and the reduction of ignorance – something I am very concerned about. Because the definition is concerned with two realities, judo done in a certain frame of mind could be included in such a definition of art. How does a frame of mind affect art? There is Duchamp, of course.

When he pinned a 'ready-made' urinal to an art gallery wall, he waited till the cries of protest had died down and said, 'If I say it is art, then it is art'. It is a statement difficult to refute, and perhaps that is what I have said.

Then there are the Japanese, who must have a major say on this topic. They have a word, 'jitsu', which means art, science, craft, technique, method of doing, etc.: a truly all-embracing word that saves much argument. If I were to say 'Judo is a jitsu' (which I could), then you could please yourself as to its meaning.

However, the meaning chosen can make a tremendous difference as to how the whole game of judo is presented to the potential participant. Duchamp's definition is very profound and enigmatic and worthy of much intellectual debate, but if it were chosen, it would not help the 'working man' much. The Japanese approach could be so general that it might offer mere bewilderment. A meaning like the one I use, implying study and practical experimentation, would take those who accepted it into many areas of work and training.

So, if we can agree that art is about changing reality, about creativity and originality, and there is some point of contiguity with a judo performance (not all judo performances) in relation to those qualities – however small – then perhaps we can learn something from art that will help us to improve judo training.

Gombrich, in his powerful book *Art and Illusion*, speaks of how the ever-changing shapes of clouds may have stimulated past artists. A good friend of mine, a professional artist, 'slashes' paint on a canvas and turns the picture round and round till she can 'see' (through half-closed eyes) a wild animal hidden in the undergrowth of paint. She then paints it in a little more 'clearly'. A Japanese artist encouraged his cat to urinate on his shoji (the sliding screens in a Japanese house) so that when it had dried out he could use the shapes of the stains to stimulate his imagination. Can we produce similar kinds of stimulus to generate new throwing and grappling skills? We will try through games.

Training situations

One of the main purposes of a training programme is to instil into the competitor a skilled response to various situations. These situations can be reduced to two main types.

1. The situation that is recognised, a part of past experience. It is anticipated, expected, and can be planned for. The opponent is assumed to take up certain 'standard' postures in certain circumstances, and 'standard techniques' are taught to cope with such 'set pieces'.

2. The situation which is not recognised; it is new and not a part of past experience. It has to be responded to spontaneously and the competitor has to learn how to create such a spontaneous attack action.

Kata and randori
The first situation is the normal one handled in most traditional training centres. Structured periods are set aside in which the competitors learn stereotyped throwing and grappling techniques, mostly in static situations (uchikomi). If they are lucky they may do 'uchikomi-on-the-move' and may be shown a few clever, one-off tricks in grappling situations. Nothing tactical is attempted, merely the reinforcement of the long-established. It is what the Japanese would call kata training, and is important but of limited value (see later).

The second type of situation, the unrecognised, the unknown, is very seldom attempted in any training centre. It is too difficult and too complex; too often its existence is not even realised. Yet, if the development of throwing skills is to move forwards, this problem must be tackled. The solution, a clue anyway, lies in unstructured training (which in judo is called randori), but so far no one has been able to utilise it in a constructive manner.

The judo fraternity is very familiar with the words kata and randori, but it has a limited understanding of what they mean. Kata, for example, is limited to a few ordained, sequential movements, accepted by everyone as sacrosanct. If they are performed and repeated often enough, it is claimed they will, in some mysterious way, improve competitive skills. It is not appreciated that the word kata has no pre-ordained connection with a specific set of sequential movements; it is merely a label to be stuck on any structured set of movements, the purpose of which is to reproduce a consistency of response to a constant situation. Kata is a very necessary part of a skill acquisition programme, but it is not the only one.

Randori, on the other hand, is totally unstructured learning; as the word describes, it is chaotic and violent. From the shambles it is hoped that new skills will emerge – spontaneously. Such a hope is based upon the esoteric truism that creativity is stimulated by chaos, not order (see later).

However, because these two training methods are so poorly understood, their intentions of consistency and spontaneity (each complements the other in the training programme) are frequently confused when implemented to improve skill. Kata is made so rigid it destroys consistency of thinking, and instead produces mindless repetition, while randori is made so competitive it destroys creative spontaneity and generates destructive development that minimises skill growth.

Consistency and spontaneity

Consistency and spontaneity are the yin and yang of skill production. Both must be trained with equal conscientiousness. It may appear that consistency is easier to develop than spontaneity (which is why many coaches spend all their time on it), but consistency is not everlasting repetition of the same thing (that is boredom). Consistency is the ability to reproduce the *same kind* of response to the *same kind* of situation, with the *same kind* of success every time. Repetition is a part of that process, but is not necessarily a dominant part.

Spontaneity may appear to be much harder to develop. There are no fixed 'hooks' of repetition on which learning can be hung. Like life itself, progress is made in mysterious quantum jumps across empty chasms of intention. By structuring non-structured situations, by mentally preparing the competitor to react spontaneously to unforeseen circumstances, he may be helped to cope with similar situations in major competitions. How can we try to do that? Through games!

Games and training

Judo of course is itself a game.

Game = a diversion, pastime, piece of fun; a contest played according to rules and decided by skill, strength or luck.

Oxford Illustrated Dictionary

So, we are really talking about sub-games, parts of a total game that is judo.

When I introduced the idea of playing games in a training session back in the mid-'sixties, judo was treated very seriously, almost religiously, so the degree of levity that was introduced along with such games was eyed with great suspicion. But gradually their value was recognised, and now they are an accepted part of most programmes.

Types of game

There are four main types, each having its own purpose.

1. **Fun games** are used intentionally to lighten the mood of the session. I do not think learning is at its best in the solemn atmosphere of a church, so they are intended to generate laughter and enjoyment. At the same time, however, I do bury in them certain elements that I want to appear in the judo performance, e.g. flexibility and morality.

2. **Training games** introduce the trainees to the 'mystical' elements in judo skills. I know, for example, that the best performers have a sense of rhythm, of design. They know where they are – both in a personal sense – upside down, right way up, position of arms and legs (body awareness) – and also in terms of location within the fighting area. They are able to anticipate the opponent's actions, and are therefore able to 'head him off at the pass'. They can change their style to suit changing conditions; they can read a contest like a book. However, this fighting wisdom takes many years to acquire; many years of sometimes bitter experience, much hit-and-miss pragmatism. Such knowledge is frequently vague and little understood. If these performers were asked how they knew the opponent was going to do 'that', they would probably look vaguely surprised, pause and say, 'Er, well, I did.'

Games like these are quite specific and will be limited to particular sessions in a training programme.

3. The third type of game is concerned with the development of **tactics and strategy**. It extends over time, perhaps for a whole season. Tactics are organised, sequential movements of attack and defence intended to bring about certain desired circumstances: circumstances that are usually intended for winning. In judo they can be used to achieve 'set pieces'; if fighters train in situational interactions over a period of time, they can discover how to dominate a contest by physical and psychological pressures. These tactical games are then developed into strategic games by linking different kinds of tactical games to make up 'umbrella' skills (see page 64) that can control whole tournaments.

4. The last type may be not so much a type of game as the implicit purpose of the game. It was the purpose for which Jigoro Kano (the founder of judo) invented judo. Kano saw judo primarily as a medium through which young people could be taught the necessity of morals in life. Through the stresses and strains of training and competition, the need for moral behaviour would become evident – particularly when reinforced by a teacher or coach.

After all, if such things as anticipation, pattern, rhythm and morality can be learned, why cannot they be taught? They may not be taught as well artificially as by life experience, but if the performer can be given strong enough clues through well-constructed games, he may learn these 'mysteries' more quickly.

What's in a game?

A game can be said to have three elements: fun, education (physical and moral) and ritual. Fun is to enliven the mind and make it more receptive to learning; learning is to generate a greater need for education; while ritual is to provide the consistency of structure around which education can cluster. But there is also a complex bonding which holds the three elements together – a respect for the past mixed with scepticism of the present. What has gone before is important, and the now needs questioning.

The next generations should appreciate what their predecessors have done for them – and for judo. However, they should also be prepared to question everything that is presented to them. They must be given the knowledge and the encouragement to question the training methods in which they are expected to take part. Whenever possible they should provide constructive alternatives. A game environment is a good place for the birth of honest criticism.

Now, it is not easy to be an eye and ear sceptic – unless you are born to it. It takes much practice and knowledge. One of the ways to start learning is to look critically at those fighting photographs that few others pay much attention to. With care they will tell much about two things.

1. The many kinds of 'weird' situations in which the competitors can find themselves that the structured programme has not taught them how to handle – but should have done.

2. The kind of general skill factors the competitor ought to have in his repertoire, but has not – because he has not been taught them.

Using pictures that no one else uses

Judo coaching moves along on the sticky rails of orthodox technique. It begins by having a 'grading syllabus' whereby limited, and limiting, techniques are spread out for the beginner to replicate exactly. If he deviates from those models he is judged wrong and does not progress to the next grade (coloured belt). Eventually, however, the novice does move on and attaches himself to an instructor who again emphasises the necessity for 'standard technique'. If the novice wishes to have confirmation of the need for such techniques, he may look in books and magazines for real action photographs, and sure enough, there they are, the standard techniques in fighting situations, as in *fig. 1*. This whole process generates in the novice an understanding that judo action is really just that – orthodox, recognisable and foretellable.

Fig. 1 *A 'text book' taiotoshi attempted in public competition.*

This is not true, of course. The novice, or indeed anybody else, will not be able to stick labels on many of the action pictures. The photographer, at the end of a long day snapping action shots, will pick out the few 'standard actions', breathe a sad sigh and put the rest – most of them – into the back of his drawer.

Let us take a few out from that drawer and see what we can learn from them. No doubt some of the information gathered will help us to make up the right sort of games.

Scepticism maintained

Misinformation does not only come straight from human errors of judgement. It can also come from ill-used machines. For example, stills cameras, and movies too, have become so much a part of the sport scene that their weaknesses are often overlooked. To give but one fault for each machine: the stills camera cannot show the dynamics of the action, only a frozen moment in time. It does not show the power of acceleration at the moment of maximum effort. The movie camera lacks the syncopation of the whole contest action and also omits perspective (location in depth), as it is only a two-dimensional image maker trying to represent a three-dimensional model. Because, unfortunately, the camera does exert such a powerful hold on the interpretation of action, many coaches deal only with what the camera deals with – posture and form – and omit what the camera omits – fluidity, pace, variation and mystery. Well-structured training games could go a long way to correcting such omissions.

What can 'bad' judo pictures show?

The following pictures were not selected from a great number, but even from that number, the nine chosen show an amazing commonality.

They capture moments in time, so conclusions drawn from such pictures must be speculative. However, if the observer is experienced, educated guesses can be made as to how the scenarios started and how they might end.

The pictures were very randomly selected: the single criterion was 'unusual'. Somewhat unexpectedly, on examination there is a remarkable similarity between some of them, which almost automatically puts them into a classification. We do tend to group seemingly disparate objects because this makes initial understanding of the essence of those

Fig. 2 Twist and space (1)   ▶
The man on his back has tried a tomoenage (stomach throw). He has started well. His right foot has 'kicked' his opponent high in the air, but here is where it starts to go wrong. The thrower has given the opponent too much air-space, and he has already lost control of the right arm. The opponent, having quickly put his right hand on the ground, is using it as a pivot-point and the large space as an escape route. By twisting in the air so that he lands on his front, he thereby avoids a terminal score. To prevent this kind of escape opportunity, an attacker must keep the opponent close to him throughout the whole throwing action.

Fig. 2

objects easier. However, we must take care that we do not cling to that first classification long after its initial utilitarian purpose has been achieved.

Turn-outs

Figs. 2 and 3 show what appear to be well-trained turn-outs. *Fig.* 2 shows a good tomoe-nage, but the throwing action has given the opponent too much 'air time', i.e. because he has been thrown along the body, instead of across it, the man is too high in the air. The right hand is on the ground, as a pivot point, and the body is twisted around it.

Fig. 3

Fig. 3 shows what is probably a reasonable ouchi attack. The opponent frees the hands and uses them to twist the body.

There will be no score in either of these attacks, in spite of the good beginnings.

Fig. 4 shows a careless attack: good positioning but no control over the opponent's head or arms. It will be easy for the man to twist from the handstand position and land on his front (no score).

◀

Fig. 3 Twist and space (2)
The standing man has managed to achieve some result in his attempt to throw his opponent backwards. As admirable as that is, the photograph shows clearly the many mistakes he has made. Since he has tried to back up his hooking right leg by grabbing the opponent's right leg with his hand, he has sacrificed all control of his opponent's upper body. The opponent has quickly released his grip and has twisted in the unrestricted space. The other big mistake the attacker has made is shown by his left leg. The uplifted toes indicate that his body-weight is falling backwards. Not only does that prevent him from restricting the twisting action of the opponent, but it also increases the space between the two bodies. If this space is to be controlled, the head must be trapped.

▶

Fig. 4 Twist and space (3)
Here the same mistakes are being repeated, but in a forward throw. The attacker gets his hips well across the front of his opponent, lifts him and rolls him over (shown by his straight legs). That is his first mistake; it gives too much air space. He should have screwed him round and down; the opponent can easily twist in the big space available – which he is doing. The second mistake is in the lack of control of the arms or the head. That facilitates the twist-out. With the hands on the ground, the twist may even get the opponent onto his feet! As before, if twist-outs are to be prevented, and high scores made, the opponent's head must be controlled.

Fig. 4

Fig. 5

Fig. 5 shows the action of an untrained fighter. 126 has probably attacked with some kind of uchimata. For some reason he has lost control of his opponent's head and shoulders. The opponent has changed the space relationship between them and is countering. He is trying to lift and turn the man over so as to land him on his back. In desperation 126 has got his left hand down and is trying to twist out using the hand as a pivot. Apart from the risk of breaking his arm, he has not created the necessary space between the bodies by using his hips. That is the sign of the untrained contestant.

◀

Fig. 5 Spontaneous reaction
Presumably 126 started this confusion! He probably launched a very sloppy attack, where he was standing on one leg – this is a dangerous way of fighting if you are going to be sloppy! His opponent is trying to take advantage of the situation in order to counter him. However, he also has very little control. Certainly, there is no control of 126's head or arm, or indeed of his legs either, so the chances of turning 126 over onto his back are very small. Never mind, he will frighten 126 who, by putting his left hand on the mat, will be able to pivot round it and land on his front. It is a dangerous way of avoiding a high score. The loss of control, and the inability to do the right thing in such a fluid situation, suggests a lack of specialist training in both men.

▶

Fig. 6 Not so bad after all!
This is a much better performance. The attacker has kept the two bodies close, so preventing the opponent from twisting in the air. However, he has allowed some space to appear between the two sets of shoulders (by allowing some freedom of the head). The opponent has pulled his head right back, thus blocking any attempt to turn him onto his back. It means he lands on his head, and from that fixed point he pivots to land on his side. He will lose a score, but only a small one. If the match is important enough, such measures may be thought necessary, but they are drastic! Again, this points to the importance of spending time in training on 'movement in space'.

Fig. 6

Fig. 6 shows a degree of 'panic' in both contestants. The man nearest the camera has tried some variation of uchimata. It had no lift, so he has tried to compensate by rolling forwards. His opponent reacted too late and was pulled down by the roll. Only at that late stage has he begun to try a twist-out. He may well not lose a 10 or 7 point score, but will almost certainly lose 5 or 3 points.

Fig. 7

Use of body-weight

Fig. 7. Poor 'Apprehensive'; he also has tried some form of uchimata/ haraigoshi, but instead of putting his weight *into* the direction of the throw, he has allowed it to fall away to his rear. The opponent has seized the opportunity and is splattering him into the direction of that weakness. It will probably hurt!

Much the same happens in *fig. 8.* Not only has 'Moustache' made a slack attack and allowed his weight to fall back (just like 'Apprehensive'), but he has also allowed his right leg to bend – which ensures that the body-weight is pulled out of the throwing-dynamic. Worse still, his panic has frozen him into immobility (he should be twisting out at this stage). Lack of movement is very dangerous for any competitor. The opponent, in spite of the expression of his face, is very pleased about that, and is driving 'Moustache' into the ground – probably for a small score.

◀

Fig. 7 Body-weight (1)
Use of body-weight was mentioned in connection with fig. 3 where the lifted toes indicated that the body-weight was falling backwards instead of moving forwards. If a competitor must use an attack that consists mainly of standing dangerously on one leg, he must understand fully the use of connected body-weight. It is no good attacking with the body-weight balanced precariously on the top of one leg – the opponent will quickly destroy such a fragile structure by hurling the attacker in the opposite direction to that in which he wants to go (as in fig. 7). The standing leg must be outside the body base/hips, opposite the direction in which the throw is being made. If that is done, disasters can be avoided. If the attacker is driven in the direction of the intended throw by the supporting leg, then even if it fails the attacker will not be scooped up and dumped on his back for a big score.

▶

Fig. 8 Body-weight (2)
This photograph shows much the same as fig. 7, but instead of the opponent throwing the attacker backwards, he is crushing him downwards so that he can start (probably) newaza (ground grappling). It shows another hazard, which compounds the big mistake of balancing the body-weight on one leg, and that is turning the back on the approach! After all, the opponent has both feet on the mat, which is a very strong and stable position. The attacker, unable to see what he is doing (!), waits to be countered. If the attack is done well, the opponent's body should be largely in front of, not behind, the attacker.

Fig. 8

▶

Fig. 9
*This photograph is similar to fig. 6, but here the attacker has
got the standing leg in the right place, i.e. outside the opponent's feet, and is driving forwards. However, he has still lost
control of his opponent's head and shoulders, which has
allowed too much space to develop between the two bodies.
Because of that, the opponent has pulled his left side out of the
action, thereby destroying any chance the attacker may have
had of turning him onto his back. The attacker was probably
holding the opponent's left collar, instead of the left sleeve,
with his left hand. Such a grip does, of course, give complete
freedom to the opponent's left arm and side. It is a mistake that
top, experienced performers make. To ensure rotation, the
outside arm/sleeve must be pulled tightly into the attacker's
body.*

In *fig.* 9, what might well have been a strong opening attack is now a disaster. The thrower has lost control of the opponent's head and outside arm (his left). That means, of course, that he will not be able to turn the man over in order to score. They will probably just crumple into the ground together – no score.

Fig. 9

Fig. 10

Fig. 10 Grappling break-outs
General principles must apply in both throwing and grappling situations. Just as in throwing actions, the control of the space between the two bodies is also extremely important in general ground wrestling. In each case, space has first got to be made to give the attacker room to move into the attack, and then it has to be closed so that maximum power can be applied to the opponent to achieve the necessary end. Fig. 10 captures the moment after the space has been closed. The power from the legs has been used to 'throw' the opponent off, and so prevent a pin being applied.

◀

Space making

Fig. 10 may have started as a throwing attack. However, I do not think so; it is ground-grappling (katamewaza).

The man underneath is making space between the bodies so that he can move and generate power through the twist of the body from the right foot. If the bodies are too close, the opponent will get a warning long before the man underneath has time to produce the twist to get him out of the pin attempt (osaewaza).

Some general principles

So, what can we learn from these brief looks at 'bad' judo photographs?

1. Fighting action must not be stopped. Once the referee says 'go' (hajime), movement must be continuous, not frantic or nervous, but positive and constructive in intent.

2. There must be flexibility in the mind as well as in the body.

3. Twisting in the air is very important, both in throwing and grappling situations. It can be a dangerous skill if left to the 'instinct' (untrained). The skills must be developed carefully, so that the competitor knows how, when and why he moves in the way he does.

4. The importance of 'anchor' and 'pivot' points must be learned. When twisting in ground-grappling (katamewaza), the various twists can only come from fixed points (hands gripping kit or on the floor). The same principle applies in standing attacks.

5. In either throwing or grappling situations, controlling the opponent's head is very important: lose the head, lose the attacking initiative; control the head, control the range of body movement.

6. Body-weight must be a fluid part of the whole attacking action. It must be driven into the direction of the throw; by so doing the bouncing power of the legs will be maximised. The attacker 'jumps' into the attack and as the feet hit the ground the leg(s) will thrust the body forwards.

If we can accept these and other principles that other sources will throw up, we shall have a base upon which to build a comprehensive and well-formulated training programme. Such sources will be found in other sports and skills (e.g. dance and arts) and in research undertaken in departments of higher education. The conscientious coach cannot afford to overlook any possible source of information that may contribute to his store of knowledge. But as gladly as he welcomes all this new material, he must put it all through his sieve of scepticism. Is it really as good as it looks? Has the researcher really found something new or merely something he was already looking for?

The coach has two major responsibilities that he must try to carry out to the best of his ability:

1. To ensure, wherever possible, that his sport retains its integrity.

2. To protect the youth in his care from destructive exploitation – be it from machines, other coaches, teachers, administrators or parents.

What about scoring?

The essential purpose within a judo contest is to score points. That is what every aspiring top competitor tries to do (or is it?).

He visits the market stall of techniques, tries many of them, selects three, four or five for his own private use and practises them to make them his own. Armed with these skills he hopes to score points and win victories. He may be quite successful at it – up to a point.

Then there is the other side of the coin – how not to lose points. He must learn how to fall (be thrown) but not lose points. In short, he must learn how to twist in the air, so that he lands in such a way that no score is conceded. When I introduced this defensive skill back in the 1960s it was met with derision and horror. Not only did it prove that the 'art of ukemi' (falling) was *not* necessary for the acquisition of throwing skills (as some rather extreme 'traditional' textbooks advocated) but also was somehow unsporting because it stopped perfectly good throws from scoring any points. Bad show!

When it was realised, however, that the twist-outs I was advocating were quite safe – if taught correctly – they were accepted readily enough. More importantly, soon after that it was realised that they gave the competitor another chance to win the match. That had to be good. Later still, a further advantage was registered: it helped to make the contests much more exciting.

Any kind of twist-out is a type of gymnastic movement. It will demand a gymnastic type of training, including such basic movements as hand-springs, cartwheels, arab springs, handstands and tumbling sequences. They should all have a place in the following games.

How to use games

Having decided what judo games are for, the next decisions are when and how to use them. First, there are the fun and factors' games – they deal with speed, strength, etc. Then come the important tactical and strategical games that have to be included in the overall plan. For example, if a six-month build-up programme were being organised, leading up to some major tournament, the tactical games would not remain the same throughout that half-year period. They would develop strategically; at the beginning the structure would no doubt be tight, and then as time passed such structures would be loosened off to bring about 'normal' competitive conditions before the tournament itself.

Warm up

The 'fun games' do not pose much of a problem, for they can be used at any time. They can be used during a particular session to alleviate some accumulated boredom, or as part of the warm up (or warm down) session, to get the trainees in the right frame of mind. No two warm up sessions should ever be the same, of course.

The warm up period has become, quite rightly, a very important part of the training session. In my young days it was given very little consideration. We simply started and got violent gradually. I must admit that, to me, warm up is still largely a psychological matter. For a young deer, lazily drinking at some quiet water hole, who suddenly senses a lion breaking cover, hurtling towards him with every intention of converting him into a take-away lunch, there is no choice. There is no time for warm ups; he is instantly in full, violent flight, prepared to risk torn muscles in preference to the lunch appointment. To be fair, however, I do not know if any research has been done in this area of stress injury. I would suspect that there is very little academic mileage on the subject of 'Muscular trauma in the male deer, when avoiding take-away meals' at any technical conference. I would speculate that the deer is in a permanent state of psychological warm up.

So it is with people: if the life they live before the training session is vastly different from that in the training session, they may well need a lengthy period to get themselves in the right mood. In this case the warm up will need many ingredients that are essential in the judo session, e.g. flexibility games, power games, controlling two body-weights games, etc. Sometimes, if the group is psychically warmed up (as young people

32

can be) no special warm up preparation is needed – they will already be excited and ready to go. So, all that has to be done is to make the first phase of the session a graduated one.

There is another aspect of warm up (and games) that is frequently overlooked and should therefore be mentioned. It is a very strong bonding agent within the group. Judo, because it is a contest between two individuals, is usually considered to be an 'individual sport'. That can be extremely misleading. Judo is much more a group sport than even judo people realise. Most of the top performers I have known always like to be surrounded by their group peers and friends, both in training and particularly in competition. I remember a psychologist asking an ex-champion why he had kept on competing (and frequently winning). His unexpected reply was, 'I wanted to stay with the lads. I enjoy their company and the only way I could ensure that would continue happening was to win'. The psychologist could hardly believe his ears!

The Japanese are very much aware of this aspect of warm up, so much of their exercises have little to do with 'mental preparation', but all to do with 'bonding'. Everything is done by numbers, and everyone in the group does his share of the counting. It does encourage a camaraderie that is not always found in European groups. But then Japan is a group society. I do not think such a bond-bias warm up would work well elsewhere.

Finally, I must add a cautionary note. I have frequently noticed when watching training sessions that warm up is used far too often as an excuse to avoid doing skill training. In an hour's training I have seen twenty-five minutes used up by the 'warm up'. To make matters worse, the exercises are sometimes so severe that the members of the group are so exhausted they are in no state to learn judo skills – the whole reason they are training! To make the bad worse, the exercises have nothing to do with judo and simply coagulate the whole thinking processes. Of course, it is so much easier – for the coach – to impose pointless exercises on the group under the guise of a 'warm up' than it is to think of games and systems that will improve skills.

Organising games

As I have given a cautionary note to the misusers of warm up, it is only fair that I should do the same for organisers of games. It should be remembered, and kept well in mind, that there is a 'law of transference'. This law says roughly, 'When skill training is done in one environment, with the intention of transferring that skill knowledge to a different environment for performance purposes, the degree of transference is proportionate to the similarity of the two environments'.

For example, when I was in the 'swimming business', trying to get that last jump to national standard, coaches used to teach people how to swim by laying them on a bench. When they could co-ordinate the arms and legs in a breast stroke action they were declared 'swimmers'! They were then transferred to the water – where they promptly drowned! The learning and performing environments were so different, there was no transference of skill.

This kind of thing often happens in 'mini sports'. The skills learned in the mini game do not transfer well into the major game, because they are essentially different.

The judo game organiser must try to ensure that there is a recognisable link between training and performance environments. They do not always have to be close, although of course the closer the better. As long as the link is there and has been thoughtfully designed, then the games should be beneficial.

Flexibility

It is always a good idea before starting any kind of strenuous exercise to do some flexibility training. The greater proportion of limb-joint injuries occur in the outer limits of the joint range; therefore, it is advisable to keep that extreme range flexible and strong. The idea is to take the joint to its fullest ordinary range, pause, relax all the muscles, push a little, pause, relax the muscles, and so on. For example, when touching the toes: bend over as far as you can go without stretching at all. Stay there, relax all your muscles, pause, bend a little further. Stop, relax, pause, push a little further. Repeat till the fingers reach the ground!

A warning: do not 'beat' into the end of the joint range. Many fighters raise their bent arms, with shoulders high, and twist the trunk as far as they can and then bang, bang, bang, in the hope that it will make their back more flexible. It will not! The muscles controlling the range of trunk twist will naturally tighten to avoid injury – remember injuries are more common in the extreme ends of the joint range – and so this will decrease the range, not extend it. In spite of the natural care the body takes of itself, injury can still occur if the 'banging' is violent enough!

Stretching must be done carefully. Stretch as far as is comfortable, pause, relax, and stretch slowly. Go through all the joints: legs, arms, trunk and head.

Games for individuals

The games in the following chapters were largely devised when I was Chief National Coach to the British Judo Association. However, they have been improved since then and others have been added. Certainly they are not exhaustive in any way. Indeed, I hope other coaches will use them as a catalyst to devise games of their own and produce the kind of skills they require for their trainees: skills that will make judo more exciting to watch and more beneficial to the participants.

The games are not in any order of performance. They simply cover certain areas that need to be developed for contest judo.

Awareness of body-weight

Awareness of body-weight is a useful factor for counter throws. The group pair off and spread round the mat. One person jumps on another's back (pig-a-back). On the word 'Go!', he clambers round the front of the standing man and back to the beginning without touching the ground. They change over, and the game is repeated.

For a group challenge, the idea is to see which pair can complete the task first. As a race, all pairs are on one side of the mat. On the word 'Go!', the standing trainee walks forwards across the mat with his partner clambering round him. The whole thing is repeated by both individuals as they move across. The winning pair is the first one to cross the mat twice.

The purpose of these games is to develop the ability to handle moving body-weight.

Another variation uses the same starting position, but this time the person on the back gets down, with the help of the standing partner, between the man's legs, up the other side and back to the starting position. He must not touch the ground. The partner repeats this.

The game can be played as a group challenge. The winning pair is the first one to complete the manoeuvre when they are standing still or when they are moving.

Starting

This is not so much a game as an exercise in keeping alert. The whole group begins by walking anywhere about the mat. There must be no general direction. Gradually the pace is quickened, but the group still moves in mixed directions. The pace is slowly increased until all are running. *Nobody must touch anybody with anything at any time.*

Because judo is a group activity, it is beneficial to all concerned that individuals are trained to 'feel' and avoid other individuals on the mats. It avoids contact injury and maximises the use of mat space.

Slipper tag

Everyone tucks a slipper into the back of their belt (behind). On the word 'Go!', everybody starts chasing other slippers. The winner of the game is the person with the most slippers at the end of a set time limit.

The game can be repeated with trainees hopping instead of running.

Hopping tournament

The mat is divided into 6ft (2m) squares. If you have a Japanese tatami type, there is no problem; if you don't have access to one, use your initiative! Each player folds his arms across his chest and tries to bump people out of their squares. If a player is knocked out, he loses. The winner is the last player left standing.

The purpose of this game is to strengthen the legs for throwing.

Pair work

Arm bounce

Both players face each other in a press-up position (see *fig. 11*). The idea is to see who can knock the supporting arms out of position first. Both players can move around as fast as they like, trying to avoid the other's attacks.

This game gets away from the boredom of press-ups, but also makes it a more dynamic 'exercise'/game. The purpose is to increase shoulder strength for pulling.

Fig. 11 *Arm bounce. Use tactics; for example, attack on the inside as well as on the outside, or attack your opponent's left with your left. In other words, go for the unexpected!*

Bounce runs

Both players start from one side of the mat. One person is on his hands
and knees. His partner stands next to him, facing the same way. The
hands-and-kneeler starts walking to the other end of the mat; the partner
bounces/jumps over him, keeping up with him as he moves.

The crawler can move faster. The partner uses one leg and then the
other to hop over him. There can be races – who takes the least time to get
to the other side of the mat, or who takes the most time. See *fig. 12*.

This is good for bounce in the legs, which is very necessary for most
throwing actions, and also helps grappling.

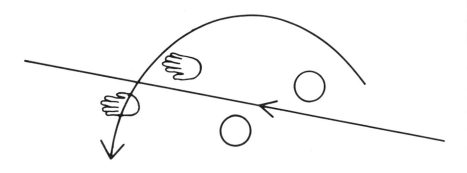

*hopping to the left, over
a partner*

Fig. 12 *Bounce runs*

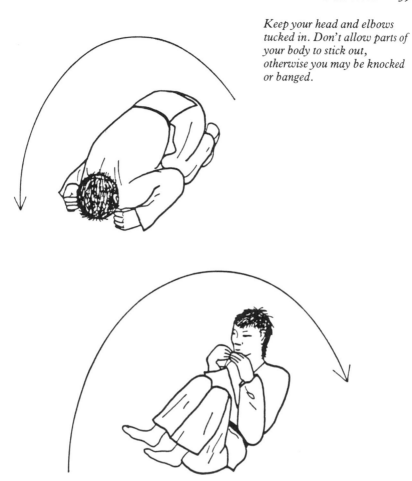

Keep your head and elbows tucked in. Don't allow parts of your body to stick out, otherwise you may be knocked or banged.

Fig. 13 *A forward roll and a backward roll*

Revolving

It is important that trainees acquire the experience of rotation in as many ways as possible. It helps them to react quickly when they find them-selves in 'strange positions' (see photographs). They should learn to do forward rolls and backward rolls (see *fig. 13*), long arm cartwheels and short arm cartwheels, and arab springs (see *fig. 14*). Long arm cartwheels are usually used for throwing situations (different kinds of twist-outs) and short arm cartwheels for grappling situations (turning out of escapes from pins/osaewaza).

A long-armed cartwheel

A short-armed cartwheel

An arab spring

Fig. 14

The whole group takes up a position on one side of the mat. The fighters move across the mat with as great a mixture of rolls and cartwheels as possible, e.g. front roll, cartwheel, back roll, arab spring, short arm cartwheel.

In competitive games, the idea is to see who can do the most revolutions in the shortest distance, or who can make the most complicated sequences.

Competition in observation involves getting an individual to do as complicated a set as he can. The rest of the group must copy it. The winner is the one who makes the most accurate copy. This is not so much an exercise in copying as in observation. It helps to train the eye to see what it is looking at – not what it thinks it ought to see.

If the facility is only a small mat, this game will not be of much use. However, big mat areas are becoming more common these days, and if they are available the use of very space-consuming, dynamic, gymnastic movements can be exploited with great value.

Monkey runs

One person assumes a press-up position, with his legs apart. The partner gets underneath, with his head between the legs. He then crosses his legs over his partner's shoulders and holds on to his belt. See *fig. 15*.

The trainee 'runs' to the other end of the mat and they roll over. The person underneath 'locks' on and his partner runs back. Exciting races can be devised with this combination.

This game is good for ground-wrestling newaza, moving two body-weights.

Fig. 15 *Monkey runs – good practice for ground wrestling. Hold on tight, since it can be a bumpy run! The secret of winning races is to achieve a quick change over, so make sure you give this plenty of practice.*

Tug-o-war

Both fighters lie on their backs, feet towards each other. A third belt or a strong piece of rope (belts can break under this kind of stress) ties their two belts together. On the word 'Go!', both start crawling away from the other, using feet and elbows. See *fig. 16*.

*partners
pull strongly
in opposite
directions*

Fig. 16 *Tug-o-war*

Having been tried that way, the game can be reversed and done the other way up. See *fig. 17*. The players are on hands and knees, they tie their belts together, and on the word 'Go!' they both start crawling.

*after tieing
their belts
together, partners
crawl away from
each other*

Fig. 17

In another variation, the belts are left tied together. The pair 'belly down' on the ground and try walking forwards on their elbows only. See *fig. 18*.

These tug-o-war games are very good for grappling power (newaza).

Who is the quickest off the mark?

The pairs move around the judo mat as if they were doing normal competitive training (randori). Each trainee is labelled A or B. At any time the person in charge of the game shouts out 'A' or 'B'. Instantly, both let go of the other's jacket and the person called out drops on to his hands and knees and scrambles/runs to the nearest (mat) edge as fast as he can. The other person must catch him before he reaches the edge. He must then turn him over on to his back and at least start a pin/osaewaza, even if he is not able to finish it. Of course, any attacking technique will do. The winner is the one who succeeds in doing what he has to do, i.e. get to the edge (before being caught) or secure the pin.

Fig. 18 *Crawling on elbows. The elbows can be used alternately, in a 'walking' manner, or together. To make the game even harder, another person may lie on each of the 'tuggers'.*

The game has several purposes:

1. It makes the players aware of where the edge is while they are moving, which is an essential element in any competitor's bag of wisdom.

2. It mentally prepares the players, making them ready to react instantly to an outside signal or cue.

3. It teaches them how to apply techniques in the hassle of action (not in the artificiality of static learning).

4. It tells them that the technique used is decided by the situation, not the situation by the technique.

It is assumed, of course, that the trainees have been given some advice and suggestions as to how to tackle this kind of problem in general. The following are a few examples.

1. Grab the collar and belt, lift the person off the ground, flip him over.

2. Grab a leg, pull him back, use the legs to turn him over.

3. Grab an arm, use it as a lever, push it up his back, so turning him over.

4. Straddle him, hook the feet into his groin, catch the collar and an arm, turn him over. See *fig. 19*.

Remember, it is better to teach generalities than specifics. It is the trainee's job to work out his own specifics.

A different form

The start is the same as above. The pair move around, as if in normal randori, but with no attacks. Again, each player is labelled A or B. On the shout of 'A' or 'B', the called individual drops on to *one* knee and then stands up quickly. Both retain grips on the jackets. On the instant the knee touches the ground, the other person must try to throw his partner – as he is kneeling or about to get up.

As with the previous game, the trainees must have been given some advice on how to tackle the problem. Here are some brief suggestions.

1. Try uchimata on the raised knee.

2. Try osoto on the raised knee.

3. Try taiotoshi on the knee that is on the ground.

4. Try sasaitsurikomihiza on the knee that is on the ground.

Keep the space between the bodies very small. This ensures better control.

Fig. 19 *Turning an opponent over in 'Who is the quickest off the mark?'*

Later, in the same created situation, the following may be tried:

1. Kansetsuwaza and shimewaza (arm locks, strangles).

2. Convert the situation into a pinning/osaewaza one.

A *challenge*: discover who can find the most unusual solution to the problem.

The purpose of this game is to generate an instantaneous response to a fleeting moment of opportunity.

Fig. 20 *Tumbling practice to improve mobility*

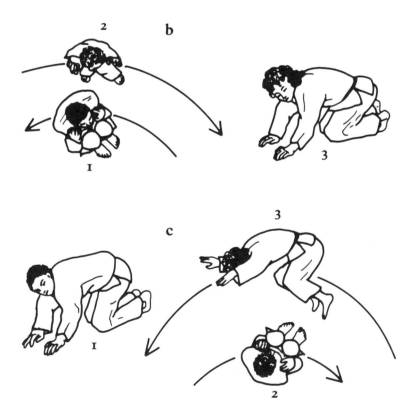

Mobility

The trainee has to think and move fast in response to an ever-changing situation. Much can be learned from tumbling.

1. Trainees kneel down, in threes (*fig. 20a*).

2. On the word 'Go!', the middle person rolls to his right (*fig. 20b*).

3. The outside person jumps over him, lands in the middle and immediately rolls towards the other outside trainee (*fig. 20c*).

4. This one immediately jumps over him and rolls sideways. The outside player jumps over him (*fig. 20d*).

The action is maintained as long as necessary, sometimes getting faster, sometimes slower.

A more 'advanced' form is shown in *fig. 21*. Here the pattern is the same, only now it is done in a standing position. The person in the middle starts the action by a forward roll to the person at the end, who does an astride jump over him. The roller finishes in a standing position and turns to face the middle. Meanwhile, the astride jumper forward rolls, while the third trainee astride jumps over him, landing in the middle. The roller bounces to his feet, turns and waits for his next action. The person in the middle rolls forwards – and so on.

d

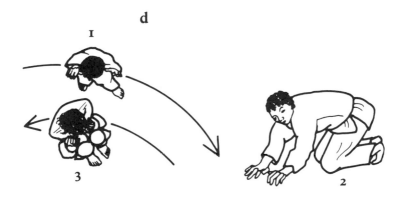

Fig. 21 Advanced tumbling practice

Scoring games

Scoring is the core of competitive judo. It decides who wins or loses. It is therefore strange to discover that it is extremely rare for score training to be included in any training session. I always teach scoring methods on the first evening of a novice's judo life. Many judo performers are not really introduced to scoring until they reach brown belt (1st kyu).

Before we start looking at some ways of learning how to score through scoring games, let me make sure the reader has a superficial knowledge, at least, of what the throwing scores consist. There are four, as follows.

10 points (Japanese ippon)
This score terminates the contest and unquestionably shows the winner – the individual who scored 10. The loser must land fully on the back for this full score.

7 points (wazaari)
The loser of the points must have landed on the side for this score to be achieved.

5 points (yuko)
The fighter thrown must land largely on the back, but this throw will lack the speed and force of a full ippon value throw.

3 points (koka)
The competitor thrown lands only on the thigh or buttocks, but with speed and force.

Game no. 1

One trainee gets on to his hands and knees, the other stands beside him (*fig. 22*). The latter holds on to the kneeler's clothes on the side nearest him. Tucking his head in on the other side, he rolls directly over, using his hand hold to control the speed of the roll (*fig. 23*). Landing on his back, he is told, would be a loss of 10 points (ippon). He should feel it and remember it.

Some time later, the same start is used, but as he rolls over the partner – using his hands as 'pivot points' – he twists in the air so that he lands on his side. This is a loss of 7 points (wazaari). He should feel and remember it.

The feet should hit the ground before the body does. The head should not touch the mat at all.

Fig. 22

The kneeler should keep his knees wide apart, so making the position very stable.

Fig. 23

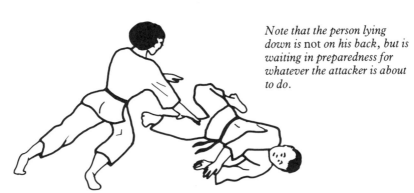

Note that the person lying down is not *on his back, but is waiting in preparedness for whatever the attacker is about to do.*

Fig. 24 *Starting position*

The game is the same for the other two low scores: roll, twist in the air, landing as appropriate for the respective score. The twists must be done to both the left and the right.

Later on the pair can move around the mat freely. At any time, the selected person can drop to his knees with no warning at all, calling out any one of the four scores. The other must quickly roll over the back of his partner, making the called-for point loss – 3,5,7 or 10.

The number of times each individual will need to practise the various rolls and scores is dependent upon ability and experience. It does not take many weeks before the landing position is easily recognised and remembered for what it is. The fighters should then be able to keep their own score in competition.

More twist-outs

One trainee lies half on his back (*fig. 24*). (When training, the participants should never lie flat on their backs. It is the position of losing, and it should never be experienced – from choice!) The partner does short-arm cartwheels over him, landing on his front, ready for a pinning attack. Both sides should be experienced, but it is best to turn over the head end, so the entanglement with the legs is avoided. See *fig. 25*.

Once these simple twist-out skills have been learned, they can be experimented with in gentle, real-life throwing actions.

Fig. 25

Competitions can be organised as to who can twist out in the best style, in the most imaginative way or in the most difficult of circumstances.

When the trainee is familiar with these twist-outs that reduce scores, he can try the one that avoids any kind of score loss. He should go back to the beginning. The person rolls over, but he twists completely so that he lands on his front (*fig. 26*). He should immediately counter-attack the partner on his knees, turn him over and pin. The idea is to attack just at that moment when the opponent thinks he is in a strong, winning position. To have to defend at such a time is psychologically very difficult.

Fig. 26

Close your legs to twist your body and to enable you to land on your feet.

Tactical games

Tactical games are not, of course, for novices. They assume that there is some understanding of attacking principles and situation responses. A brief indication of what is meant by 'principles' and 'responses' is given below, so that performers will understand what they should know before they start playing the following games.

Attacking principles

These are usually learned through the teaching of throwing and grappling attacks. Once the standard form has been taught, the following principles would be stressed as the grapples, throws, etc. are being practised.

When throwing:

1. after making a body contact with the opponent, make sure the attacker can *increase* the throwing force, not *lose* it

2. get the inside, power leg *behind* the direction of throw

3. make sure the attacker can *push* the opponent into the ground, not *pull* him into the ground.

When grappling:

1. when pinning, the attacker must control the opponent's head

2. to break out of any attack the attacker must make more space between the bodies, so that he can move and get momentum

3. the attacker should not use 'dead end' skills, i.e. ones which leave the fighter with nothing if they fail. If the opponent avoids the first attack, the attacker must have something with which to follow up.

Situation responses

These are seldom taught in judo clubs. The idea is to instil into the trainee the importance of pace change and knowing where he is in the fighting area. These are essential ingredients of competitive judo skills, and therefore the earlier the aspiring judo player learns them, the better.

Pace change

One way of teaching this is to divide the training mat area into 12ft (3.6m) squares (bigger or smaller depending on the overall mat size). See page 36.

Label each square fast, slow or medium pace, in a haphazard manner. As the players move around the squares they must change their pace (of movement) according to the pace indicated by the square. The labels must not be kept in the same squares for long.

Once the players have learned how to change pace in this rather rough classification of three (some champions I have known can fight at eight different paces), they can then be taught which throwing and grappling attacks suit each pace. The following are some examples.

Throws
Fast – haraigoshi, ashi-waza, osoto gari, tewaza.
Medium – uchimata, hiza-guruma, osotogake.
Slow – ipponseoi, ukiwaza, taiotoshi.
N.B. If throwing style is changed, so should pace, e.g. if haraigoshi is converted into a hip throw, instead of a leg throw, it can be done at a medium pace.

Grappling
Fast – arm locks.
Medium – strangles.
Slow – pins.

It is a simple correlation and therefore not always true, but it is an adequate start and should help competitors to appreciate change of pace. This is essential for combination attacks.

Location awareness

Let the players move around the outside squares. Let them feel how the contest edge constrains them on one side, but gives them maximum freedom on the inside. Let them move around the inside squares and feel they have no restrictions at all on any side. Show which kinds of attacks can be executed on the outside squares and which ones on the inside. The outside ones are those in which the direction of attack is easiest to control, e.g. the back throws, taiotoshi, whereas the middle squares are for those attacks that are not primarily concerned with direction, e.g. ipponseoi, sutemiwaza.

Armed with those basic ingredients of skill acquisition, let us move on.

Registering the edge

Both players stand in the middle of the official fighting area, 30ft × 30ft (9m × 9m). They walk together several times to the four compass point edges of the mat. They then walk to the diagonals several times. Some extra movements are added before getting to the edge. All the time, put sensitivity into the body so that it can *feel* where the edge is; the soles of the feet become sensors and can 'recognise' the edge. Next, one trainee shuts his eyes and the other steers him round, eventually getting to the edge before the other tells him he is there.

The moves are gradually made more complicated, always ending at the edge. The 'blind man' should always be asked if he can find the edge first.

The time needed to achieve this edge-sensitivity naturally varies from individual to individual. It is a very useful skill to have, and although it may sound difficult to achieve, most people I have trained this way could do it eventually, and effectively.

Anticipation

This is probably the most difficult quality to train in the individual. For some lucky people it will be there, waiting all ready to be 'picked up' and exploited. Others will need to work hard at it for some time before they acquire confidence in their ability to handle this factor.

There are natural counterers, people who have an innate speed or a particular sort of reflex that allows them to counter even the most effective attacks. They are fortunate, and will win most of their contests in this way. Seldom will they win by imagination or original attacks, but then that is often how they live their lives, too, so it is not unexpected.

The more enviable person is the one who can stop the attack before it even starts. That is why a match between two highly skilled fighters can appear so boring to the spectator, because nothing seems to be happening. Each attack is stopped before it is launched.

The Japanese have a word for it: go-no-sen. It means something like 'before the moment'. Originally it was used by swordsmen (kennin), and meant that the best time to parry the sword cut was 'before the moment' it was taken out of the scabbard. In other words, the sword was to be prevented from even being drawn. There are many *Samurai* stories telling of how the master swordsman won a duelling challenge in this way, e.g. rowing across to an island where the duellers could fight in private: the master politely offering to let the challenger disembark first and then rowing away, leaving him to fight his own shadow. It is a reassuring sign that the message of the *Samurais' Bible*, the *Hagakure*, which says 'Death is the only purpose for the *Samurai*,' was not ubiquitously held throughout Japan.

The numbers' game (to develop anticipation)

The following game can easily be organised as a two-team match. The winner is the first team which has all its members achieving the set objectives. Let me start by describing what each pair has to do.

A trainee from each team is labelled A or B. One is chosen to start the first phase. He moves around the mat as if in free play. B, the chosen one, must silently and repeatedly count up to twenty. When he is ready, he selects any number between one and twenty, and on that number, e.g. eight, he attacks A. It is a good attack, but he omits the final throwing-down action. B keeps repeating the attack (any attack), but on the same number every time, i.e. eight. A must try to guess what that number is. When he thinks he has guessed it, he stops moving. He waits till the rest of his team have also stopped.

In the next phase, B continues with the same intention as before – to attack on the number eight. However, A must now attack on the previous number, i.e. seven. After several repetitions they can stop and confirm with each other whether or not A has guessed correctly. If he has, they wait till the rest of A's team have done the same. If A has guessed wrongly, they will have to start again from scratch.

It may turn out that A guesses the right number, but at a different rate from B's counting. For example, B is attacking on eight, but A will be counting twice as fast or at half the speed, i.e. four or sixteen, and will therefore attack on three or fifteen. This does not matter; it is the rhythm of anticipation which is important.

The phases can be timed, and the team with the shortest time to have all its members through both phases successfully is the winner.

Movement patterns

The same idea can be used in terms of anticipating movement patterns. The mat is divided up into 6ft (2m) squares. B is asked to use any attack, but not successfully, on a fixed sequence of squares, e.g. every fifth. He manoeuvres A through four squares and attacks on the fifth. In the early days of the game-experience A allows himself to be so manoeuvred.

Later on, with practice, B has to make A move in his preferred pattern. When A thinks he has worked out the pattern, he stops as before. They start again, with B still attacking at the end of a fixed sequence in the fifth square. Now, of course, A attacks at the fourth square. Again, they can compare notes and learn something from the verbal as well as the physical exchanges.

Both of these games can be played in grappling. Remember, it is the *pattern* of movement that gives the clue to the moment of anticipation and so of attack.

I have known many champions who have attacking patterns of this sort. In the above game, particularly in the early days, as has been said, A allows himself to be manoeuvred from square to square. In competition, that certainly would not be the case. B would drive A from 'square to square' with various kinds of combination attacks, feints, dummy-threats and the like, but there could still be a pattern, regular and to be recognised if the ability is there in the opponent. So, the game can be played for real, and it has two purposes:

1. to make the opponent move in such a way, to be in such a posture, to move at a certain pace and to be in a particular position that facilitates the favourite attacking action of the fighter.

2. to make the opponent move in harmony with the attacker, so that he can control the attacking and defensive actions of the opponent. When the two fighters' movement patterns are antagonistic to each other, it is extremely difficult to make a winning attack. When there is harmony (of movement) between the two, winning moves are more likely.

Certainly, it is a 'game' I have often played in top class competition (which is why I modified it to fit into a training programme) – and one that has often been played on me! It is what makes some people call judo a 'physical game of chess'. It is the part of judo skills I find most fascinating and one which I enjoy the most. To be able to get 'inside the skin' of another fighter in this way and make him do what you want gives great satisfaction. It easily surpasses the pleasure of throwing down the opponent or beating him. Winning is crude compared to go-no-sen.

The strategic development of tactical games

In most forms of creative development there is a strong propensity to move from the structured to the unstructured, from the specific to the abstract. Look at many of the great artists: Van Gogh, Picasso, Chagall and of course, Turner. In their youth they were very careful and accurate 'draughtsmen'. As the years rolled by they became increasingly sep- arated from form and became concerned with feeling and spirit, which in turn is all about movement and excitement.

So it is with the judo fighter, for in his own way, he is also an artist – if he is a creative performer. He may want to be structured and to be taught 'technique' in his early novice days, but the nearer he gets to the 'top' the more 'abstract' he will wish to become. He will want his own skills with his name stamped on them; he will not wish to be constrained by other people's performances. He will want to do everything that is wrong – in the right way for him. Can we help him?

The tactical games outlined above are not just games, they are experiments, too. Because they are experiments, the results found will need to be recorded so that they are not forgotten. The experiences need to be jotted down for future reference. The artist uses his sketch book, the novelist his notebook and the judoman his kata. As he gains knowledge and experience from the games he plays, he should jot that information down in a set of short simple, sequential movement patterns. For example, if he has played the first anticipation game, he may want to make the following brief physical notes.

B (uke, in Japanese parlance) takes four steps backwards.

A (tori) attacks on the third step – as B takes his right foot back.

With a friend he could practise this in odd moments during the training programme. As the complexity of the training increases, along with that of the games, so would the complexity of the kata 'notes'.

Example 1

A (tori) attacks on change of direction: that is, B moves backwards and A feints with a taiotoshi attack. B moves forwards to stop that attack, and then A really attacks with ouchigake for a score.

Example 2

A (tori) attacks on change of pace. B moves quickly sideways (to his right), and A feints with a foot trip. B slows down to block the attack and A then really attacks with ippon seoinage.

The training schedule

It is, of course, quite impossible to describe how a whole seasonal training programme would be developed in tactical and strategical ways; not only because there is nothing like the necessary space available here, but far more importantly because we do not know the personality of the people involved.

However, let us look at a hypothetical programme and imagine we have a six-month run-up period to a major event. It is an international event, so we know roughly the standards that we can expect; therefore, we know approximately what has to be done to surpass those standards. In a real situation we would also know how much money there is available (and therefore how many training sessions can be afforded) and the distances to be travelled.

Looking at such a half-year training plan, we could call it a 'macro-view', for it would be like looking through the wrong end of a pair of field glasses: details would be so small that little sense could be made of them. It would be better if we could somehow shrink the whole six-month scheme down to a small manageable size – a 'microview' – so that we could see all the details clearly.

I would like to use the nage-no-kata as the shrinking agent. Let us try to imagine that the time it takes to learn the nage-no-kata represents the six-month training programme. The standard fifteen throws will represent *all* the throws that have to be learned and studied. They must be developed from sequential 'set piece' performances to a free, spontaneously created skill, which is just the way it would/should happen in any real training programme.

In most judo clubs, skill learning practices assume that only 5% of contest time contains unknown situations, and that 95% of any contest consists of 'set pieces', i.e. the situation must be recognised before any attack is launched.

The reality, of course, is almost the opposite. I would estimate that only about 15–20% of the fighting time is concerned with 'set pieces', while 80%–85% is full of unknown situations that must be responded to spontaneously; yet no training scheme has 'spontaneous creativity' as a part of its plan. The gradual development from tactical to strategic training should eliminate that fault.

Before we begin to look at this strategic development, perhaps I had better give a brief outline of what the nage-no-kata is and what its purposes are. Because it is a training tool, it can be made to serve many

61

purposes, some better than others. I wish to use it for a particular one, and it is for that specific purpose that I will describe it – others may wish to use it for different reasons.

The throwing action

Any throwing action can be reduced to several bio-mechanical factors which in short are:

1. the development of dynamic power through the correct use of body-weight. Production of power can take the form of a direct up-thrust from the leg or legs. As this action is directly anti-gravitational, it demands a disproportionate amount of energy to get an adequate effect. In competition, therefore, spiral thrust (downward) is preferred. It is more effective because it exploits, rather than opposes, gravity to help the action.

    In practice the aim is to generate the power. Spiral means the 'power leg' must be outside the 'hip base' so that it can drive or thrust the body into the direction of the throw – around and down.

    The 'action leg', the leg on the periphery of the downward spiral, facilitates the thrust of the 'inner' power leg, e.g. it stabilises the body twist by being put on the mat, by taking the opponent's legs out from under him, or by acting as a pivot point if the power leg has to be moved into a more advantageous position.

2. the hands (of the attacker) are the levers through which the power is transferred to the opponent. They must therefore be mechanically efficient. The hands pull the attacker's body close to the opponent, with the upper arms at approximately 45° to the body. Such a pull locks the two upper bodies together and allows the attacker's hips to get close to the opponent's body, so that when the hips twist (a part of the spiral) there is only a short gap through which the energy and power must pass.

3. the head controls the body turn (spiral). Sometimes the spiral must go through 130°, in which case the head will need to lead it all the way (as long as it 'stays in contact'). At other times, the spiral need only be a quarter turn, in which case the head limits the turn to that amount and no more.

Nage-no-kata

Now, back to the kata. Kano (the founder of judo) wanted to show how these forces and levers were applied when making up a total throwing action. He then went through a period of experimentation, trying to find the best kind of throw to show the use of the hands, hips, legs and body-weight power. For some reason which we do not know, he did not think it was necessary to show the function of the head (perhaps he simply overlooked it!). There were therefore four sections, with three techniques in each hand, hip and leg section, and six in the body-weight section. Presumably he thought that was the most important factor (and I would completely agree with him!).

The first section deals with the hands. The first throw (ukiotoshi) is traditionally done extremely inefficiently (not the way advocated by Kano, in fact). Traditionally, far too much space is allowed to appear between the bodies, making transfer of power almost impossible; therefore, the action is ineffective. The next two throws show the principle very clearly and correctly (ippon seoinage and kata guruma). Both bodies are clamped closely together. It is the hands that bring about this 'glued together' image. What should happen in ukiotoshi is that the attacker steps *forwards* with his power/inside leg, so allowing the bodies to move very much nearer each other.

The next section deals with the use of the hips. The first throw, ukigoshi, shows how the hips are used to rotate the opponent horizontally (no lift) by having the driving leg positioned outside and behind the opponent's foot base. The second throw, haraigoshi, shows again how the opponent's hips can be (horizontally) rotated (as in the first throw), but how the action leg knocks the legs out from under him. The third throw, tsurikomigoshi, demonstrates how the hips are used to lift the opponent off the ground (by straightening the legs).

The third section deals with the use of the legs. The first throw, okuriashiharai, shows how when two bodies are pulled closely together (as should happen in ukiotoshi), with the attacker's hips twisted strongly, the opponent's feet can be taken out from under him. The second throw, hizaguruma, is much like the first, but now the body twist hurls the opponent over his own fixed foot (planted firmly on the ground and trapped by the attacker's action leg). The third attack, uchimata, again reveals the need to get the bodies close with the power leg outside the opponent's foot base. This naturally drives the bodies outwards and forwards in a downward spiral, with the action leg going between the opponent's legs, swinging up, lifting the defender's leg up and so tilting him over the other leg. This reinforces the downward spiral.

The last section, divided into six sub-sections, shows various uses of a totally committed body-weight action. To describe them all in detail would take too long*, but they can be put into two groups.

1. The attacker's body-weight is driven in, under and close to the opponent's feet. The power leg drives in past (and between) the opponent's foot base and pushes him (the opponent) forwards with the power from the hips. The hands keep the opponent's head well down – so rolling him, generally, forwards, e.g. tomoenage, sumigaeshi, yokoguruma.

---

*Read my books *All About Judo* and *The Anatomy of Judo*

2. The attacker's power leg goes to the outside of the opponent's foot base, with the body up straight; the bodies are again locked together. The hips are strongly twisted, turning (not rolling) the opponent forwards, e.g. uranage, yokogake, ukiwaza.

In brief, the first attack rolls the opposition head-over-heels, while the second 'screws' him out of the ground.

At the start of the training season, the team members may well need to have these principles drilled into them by learning the fifteen throws to both the left and right (for who knows when they may want or need to change sides).

First they may need to learn the precise way the various basic factors have to be used: how the hands have to work together, pulling the attacker close to the opponent; how the position of the power leg has to change to suit the different types of throwing action.

However, such accuracy must not become a fetish. From time to time some slackness must be allowed to enter into the performance of the throw, because from the outset of the programme the trainee must realise the need to be capable of correcting errors – of action and judgement – immediately they are made, as made they always are!

The umbrella skill

Remember that a match, a contest, is a continuous interaction between two people through time. Of course, there are single skills, throws and grappling, but more importantly there is one 'umbrella' skill which oversees the whole contest. The aspiring competitor must always keep the umbrella skill in mind. Too much emphasis on single skills and too much time spent on them can destroy the umbrella skill and hence the ability to win.

So, when learning single skills, as in the nage-no-kata, they should not be seen as fifteen single separate throwing techniques, but as a stream of movement swirling over fifteen performances.

The kata speed game

To make an elementary point, play the kata speed game. Cutting out all extraneous movement, instruct the trainees to do the thirty throws (left and right) as fast as they can. When I used this game in the National Youth Squad, the record was about 3½ minutes! That's good for a warm up as well as for speed and stamina. However, it should also be remembered that if speed is emphasised too heavily, accuracy and control frequently fly out of the window. So, in the next game, do the thirty throws as slowly as possible and make sure every part of the body is in the right place every second during every throw.

Now add the dimension of movement. Initially, in order to keep the development simple, move along a straight line covering a distance of about 12–15 ft (3.6–4.5 m). Make the attacks when the opponent (uke) is moving forwards or backwards. See who can find the most attacking opportunities. Is it best if uke's feet are like this or like that? How do those changes modify the attacking form? How many variations of the one technique can be found within the form of the technique? For example, how does ippon seoi nage need to be changed if the opponent is to be thrown backwards instead of forwards?

By playing such games, by varying the basic factors of foot position, body shape, hand use and spiral range, all kept well within the limitations of a straight line movement, the participants will get to know such things as the importance of the movement between the attacking techniques, and the rhythm and flow of the action from the finish of one technique to the start of the next.

To use a 'speed kata' can have special benefits just before a match. Not only does it have the ingredients of a good warm up (incorporating as it does all the movements needed in a contest), but it also acts as a reminder of what the individual is capable of doing. It is quite surprising how often a contest is lost simply because the fighter has forgotten something he has learned in training. Just about the time I was leaving national coaching, I realised how important such a 'reminder' was, so I devised a special kata of tactics (the senjitsu-no-kata). It incorporates the many specialised skills that are used in contest, but are seldom ever taught, e.g. double bite attacks, early and late countering, linked attacks for special occasions (see my book *All About Judo*).

Unrestricted movement

Go for unrestricted movement. Keep the kata sequence as it is (throwing both left and right), but ask the players to attempt moving freely about the mat. Encourage them to feel their own style of syncopated movement. They should slide, not jerk, into the attacking movements. See who gets the feeling first. Let them try to describe it to the others. Use the squares: certain throws can be executed in specific ones. For example, A does several throws up to a particular square; then the partners change and B throws after the square. Ritual is being loosened; abstraction is just beginning.

Problem solving

Problem solving, or how to face the unexpected, is an important part of any top performer's training. Games can provide the problems – and some of the solutions. A fighter must certainly have practical working knowledge. He must know what to do when he meets a situation he knows, but he must also apply some theory so that he can instantaneously manufacture new knowledge for situations he does not know.

The game? – find the missing throw!

A and B, working as a pair, are asked to link three throwing attacks from the nage-no-kata. Two are given; they have to find the third – and provide a justification for the throw they have chosen. An example: the two stated attacks are ukiotoshi and okuriashiharai. After debate and trial and error they produce ipponseoinage. The reasoning for this is that ukiotoshi is done at a medium pace, so to avoid it B has to jump round it and move quickly away (stepping up the pace). A then follows even more quickly (he does not have to kneel down to do ukiotoshi) and attacks with okuriashi (a fast pace technique). B, to block the attack, drops the pace (almost stopping). A uses the static opportunity for ipponseoi.

This is a good sequence and a good explanation. The fighters could also be reminded that 'problem solvers' are seldom satisfied with their first results. Their best successes are made only after several attempts. As the structure of the traditional nage-no-kata is being gradually dismantled, more and more is being expected from the competitors.

Here may be a good place to expand on that obscure aspect of art and judo – space and void – which has already been mentioned briefly before. I find it a fascinating factor, the importance of emptiness in a dynamic, creative situation. The Japanese word 'kara' covers both space and void, but for me each has its place in the analysis of skills. By explaining these two factors carefully, many aspects of skill become much easier to understand – for me, any way!

Space

The space between the fighters usually decides their tactics. Little space means restrictive movement, which is good for defence and for transfer of power when a great deal of power is needed, e.g. ipponseoinage. Big space means lots of room in which to move, which is beneficial for generating momentum through movement (e.g. uchimata). However, it errodes control. Good fighters are always trying to maintain an optimum balance between these two types of space variations.

For in practical terms these two kinds of spaces affect the extent of body contact when a throw is attempted and thereby the degree of success that can be expected. For example, if the pace is slow and there is little space between the two bodies before the attack is made, then when the attack is launched, as much body contact as possible is required. Put another way, the greater the body surfaces in contact, the greater chance there is to transfer the maximum throwing power from the attacker to the opponent.

Here is another example. If the pace is fast and there is a lot of space between the bodies before the attack, then little (if any) body contact is necessary. However, in such a circumstance 'body contact' must be generated through the tension between the two bodies through that space. Hence the mystery of performance. The hands do, of course, provide the vital material link, but the tension in the void is very important. The hands on their own will not achieve success, yet I have seen throws done with no hand contact at all!

To get such tension, the space between the bodies must always be squeezed, or squashed, *not* expanded. I can give a good example of a bad illustration from the standard nage-no-kata. In ukiotoshi (the first throw), at the moment of throwing, the attacker steps back and *increases* the space between the bodies. This makes completion impossible. The attacker must step forwards, squeezing the space and so allowing the throwing force to be concluded through the tension of the void. The attacker then kneels down *after* the throw has been made.

If all the throws in the standard nage-no-kata are studied in the context of space, those that are designed correctly, and those that are not, are clearly evident. Throws such as tomoenage and uranage show how the attacker steps forwards into the throw – they are well performed. On the other hand, throws such as sumigaeshi, yokogake, yokoguruma and ukiwaza are badly performed because the attacker falls back from the opponent and allows this space between the bodies to *open*.

Coaches who do not understand the correct manipulation of the space between the fighting bodies during attack and defence will have great difficulty when it comes to helping a performer to improve his skill ability.

Void

This is a moment in a contest in which nothing happens. There may be several moments, and sometimes – not often – none at all. It happens when there is a change of movement pattern, a change from an attitude of attack to one of defence, i.e. a change of thought process. The contestant who recognises it first has a great advantage. Let us use the kata to recognise space and void.

There are three excellent examples of the void, even in traditional nage-no-kata. They are the blows: seoinage, ukigoshi and yokoguruma. The void is the 'gap' between a non-judo action – the blow – and the judo action – the throw. There are two mental processes, i.e. two attacking attitudes in different modes. One attacks with an untrained weapon, the other counter-attacks with a trained skill. The first makes the second possible, because of the void at the end of the first and the beginning of the second. I will try to make this point quite clear: when I trained in the Kodokan as a special research student, we were told we should actually physically pause at the end of the blow, although only for a mini-second. Here is the change of thought processes.

This same gap/void can be found in many throwing situations, e.g. a panic attack met by a trained counter. In the game of 'Find the gap', the trainees can try to feel it; in that gap various kinds of counters can be initiated, early or late.

Spontaneity

Again, both A and B move freely about the mat, doing the nage-no-kata sequence. The person in charge, just before an attack is to be made, suddenly shouts out the name of the technique. If it is A's turn to attack, he must stop it and immediately replace it with another attack. This may be any one, but it must be completely appropriate to the situation. B should not just let it happen, but should test the attack for its appropriateness. The fighters should discuss that attack. Next time, B must make the change of attack. Both partners should be able to utilise previous knowledge.

The game can be enlarged by someone deciding who 'invents' the substitute technique the quickest. After all, it may take some individuals several minutes to think of a substitute when they first play the game. Gradually, as they become accustomed to the pressure, they should be able to reduce the time gap to almost nothing.

Other shouts could be used to spark off other spontaneous responses, e.g. the attacks can be countered by particular types of counter. Earlier games could be used but now modified to suit the improved level of skill. For example, the first of the anticipation games could be reintroduced (see page 57) but without counting. The fighters would be expected to *know* when their opponent was going to attack. The action of go-no-sen would emerge spontaneously from the feel of the situation.

Play some bingo!

The trainees move freely around in couples. Put four labels on four table tennis balls. Drop them into a bucket – or something similar – bounce them around and pull one out. Call out the instruction; everyone must respond immediately. They will, of course, know what the labels mean before the start of the game. For example, the four labels could read as follows.

'Fast defence!'

This means that both A and B are moving fast and easily round the mat. B is using both the edge of the mat area and the central control area to limit the attacks of A. B is not allowed to attack, but he may counter. A has to work out a tactical plan to overcome this negative attitude. As soon as 'Fast attack!' is called out he must implement his plan.

'Slow defence!'

This means that B moves very 'heavily' in a crouched or semi-crouched position. He keeps the edge of the mat at his back to protect himself from any back throws. He simply 'blots' out any attack from A. A's job is to work out a plan to change the pace, get B away from the edge and attack with the appropriate type of attack to achieve a change of pace. On the shout, 'Slow defence!' he implements his plan.

'Fast attack!'

This means that both move around at a medium to fast pace. B limits his attacks to that pace (e.g. haraigoshi, ankle trips, osotogari). They should be real, i.e. if he throws A, that is acceptable. A must organise a plan to change the pace and so stop B's attack. It can be done by anticipation or early countering, or by any other means. On the shout 'Fast attack!', that is what he does.

'Slow attack!'

This means that again B is moving slowly and cautiously, attacking – for real – with only body throws (sutemi) or powerful hip throws (ipponseoi, tsurikomigoshi, etc.). How does A step up the pace in order to block these attacks? Somersault out of the falls, a rally of attacks, psychology of superiority? On the order 'Slow attack!', something like that should happen.

This kind of training puts a great deal of mental stress on the performer. As structure is being dismantled, the performer must carry an increasing load of responsibility, for organising tactical renrakuwaza (combinations). This is when he needs a good coach!

Good coaches should always be on hand, waiting to offer advice on the many solutions found and/or helping the trainees to think of more original responses. The coach needs great wisdom. If he is not careful, if he is slack in attitude and complacent in his ignorance, he will find himself offering the same advice he has been offering for many a past year! It is no longer relevant. The situations then were nothing like they are now, so if that 'advice' is given, it is nonsense! In short, the coach must be more imaginative than the performer.

Spontaneous creativity

Finally, even 'bingo' must be discarded! The trainees should be encouraged to invent their own situations and solutions as they go along, spontaneously and creatively. All attempts to structure the sessions are abandoned. Chaos and confusion is the order of the day. It is only the omnipresent coach who will prevent chaos degenerating into shambles, for only out of chaos will skill emerge.

Creativity is not, of course, about producing something out of nothing. It is the rearranging of existing pieces of knowledge and performance into different kinds of knowledge and performance: different manifestations that have not been seen before. It is usually achieved in a flash of 'insight'. An intensive study of a subject has been going on for a long time. Knowledge, experience, trial and error have been bubbling, like some intellectual cooking pot, for a long time and suddenly it boils over and that's insight! Then the cry of 'Eureka' echoes across the land! An attempt to show this kind of discovery process has been shown here. There are, of course, many other ways.

Experienced judo readers will no doubt recognise this final phase. In British judo circles it is called 'randori'. Randori means confusion, chaos, violence (in an elemental context) as opposed to kata, which means structure, organisation, predetermination. Has the reader seen Kurasawa's magnificent film *Ran*? (It is the same ideograph.) Here pure paternal love emerges from the chaos of family feudery. But there is a major difference between the traditional British randori and the type suggested here, which is achieved through a games approach. In two words, it is 'thinking style'. Because traditional randori has very little, if any, strategic training, in terms of development through time, progress is very slow. The individual is assumed to acquire competitive skills by simply being in the 'hurly burly' of 'judo practice'. It can happen, of course (as generations of judo players have proved), but it takes a long time. Many do not last the course (particularly if they are 'bright'). In the trade that is known as 'convergent thinking', meaning that thinking/action goes around and around in ever decreasing circles till it disappears – well, I will leave it to your imagination to supply the destination.

Putting performers through long-term structural programmes, where they begin by learning inductively and then move forwards towards a deductive style of learning, does provide an organised long-term approach to skill acquisition. It is not the only one, of course, by any manner of means. Another alternative, and one which could be used just as effectively, would conform to the opposite pattern: that is, start deductively and end inductively. The choice would depend upon the physical bias of the group members, their intelligence and their aspirations. We are back to the imagination and wisdom of the coach.

It is the long-term planning that is important. How are the trainees to be introduced to tactical and strategical developments? Games are certainly one way of learning these difficult umbrella skills (see page 64). Through games, the competitors may be better prepared for those many occasions in contest which have seldom been met before. This book has tried to show how training can be made to expand and broaden the mind, to encompass more knowledge – the business of divergent, original and imaginative thinking. Randori is the climax of such training, where restrictions are taken off, not clamped on by unreasonable competition. It is a time of creativity, of imagination, of aesthetic appreciation. Given the right kind of mix of these qualities a part of judo can become something of a performing art. The other, larger part, can become an excellent combat competitive system!

Mind you, not everyone would want to train in the way being suggested here. Many would prefer the old ways, the ways of dreary repetition and time-wasting randori. That's fine; let them. Everyone should be able to do what they prefer, but surely those people who need an intelligent training programme should be given the opportunity to work in one?

It is not fair to assume that all trainees wish to follow the robot-making training scheme. Some want to think, to know what they are doing and then to enjoy what they have done because that is the way they planned to do it.

Self-actualisation, getting to know how one fits into the world, is probably the most powerful motivation there is for the individual to *do* something. This is best achieved through some creative process: art, science, sport, judo. It is a process that can be done solely by the individual, but is best achieved when helped by a teacher or a coach who can point out the path: a teacher who has trained himself over many years and is still training himself to be more and more self-aware – a man who is his own severest critic.

Last of all, may I leave you with the coach's prayer:

Give me the courage to change those things that need to be changed,
The strength to accept those things that cannot be changed,
And the wisdom to distinguish between the two.

Index